Contents

Introducing Earthquakes

A major earthquake always makes dramatic headline news. On 17 August 1999, an earthquake measuring 7.4 on the Richter scale devastated north-western Turkey, killing over 20,000 people. The epicentre was at Izmit, a densely populated industrial town. Many cheaply built buildings collapsed, burying people in their homes and leaving thousands homeless. Rescue teams were called in from all over the world, but for many of those trapped beneath the rubble, help came too late.

▲ Rescue workers searching a collapsed building after the Colombian earthquake in January 1999.

A destructive force

Earthquakes are a constant threat to people, and one of nature's most destructive forces. The earth experiences more than 3,000 earthquakes each year, but only a few of these (between seven and eleven on average) cause serious damage and loss of life. An average of 10,000 people are killed each year by earthquakes, but in some extreme cases this number can be multiplied by more than twenty. In 1976, for example, in Tangshan City, China, a huge earthquake killed 240,000 of the 1 million inhabitants.

HELL HAS COME TO COLOMBIA

The tremor cut a path of devastation across a disaster zone spanning 20 towns and villages in five mountainous provinces in the country's coffee-growing belt. Emergency workers said last night they had searched less than a quarter of the devastated homes in the desperate hunt for survivors. "There are more than 1,000 dead, perhaps more than 2,000 in Armenia alone," said Ciro Antonio Guiza, the city's deputy fire chief.

Extract from *The Guardian*, 27 January 1999

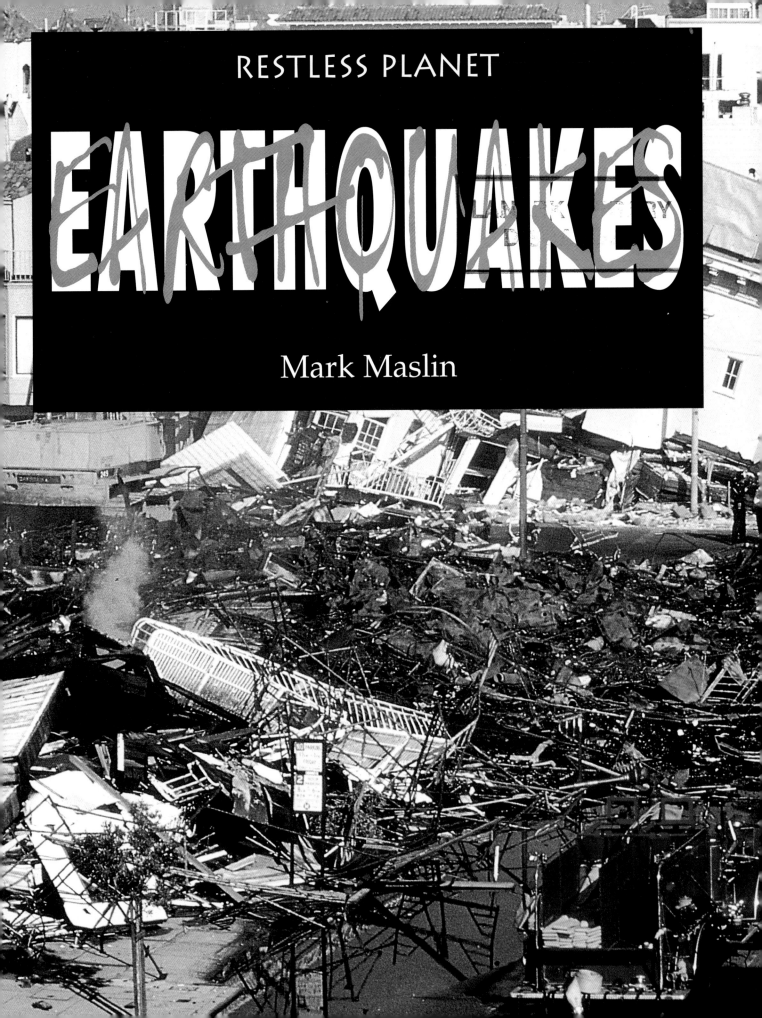

RESTLESS PLANET

EARTHQUAKES

Mark Maslin

RESTLESS PLANET

EARTHQUAKES

Other titles in this series:

FLOODS STORMS VOLCANOES

Cover photograph: Rescuers search through the debris of Acquapagana church in central Italy, which suffered heavy damage after several earth tremors hit the region on 7 October 1997.

Title page: Collapsed houses the day after the Loma Prieta earthquake in California, in October 1989.

Contents page: The San Andreas Fault crossing the Carrizo Plain in California.

Consultant: Bill Clarke, Education Officer,
The Natural History Museum
Editor: Hazel Songhurst
Series editors: Polly Goodman and Philippa Smith
Book design: Tim Mayer

First published in 1999 by Wayland Publishers Ltd
61 Western Road, Hove, East Sussex
BN3 1JD England
www.wayland.co.uk

British Library Cataloguing in Publication Data
Maslin, Mark
Earthquakes. – (Restless Planet)
1. Earthquakes – Juvenile literature
I. Title
551.2'2

ISBN 0 7502 2472 X

Printed and bound in Italy by G. Canale & C.S.p.A.

Acknowledgements
The publishers would like to thank the following for allowing their photographs to be reproduced in this book: Camera Press 4, 18t, 26, 39; Robert Harding 40; Image Select/Ann Ronan 33; Impact 27; PHOTRI 22, 24; Popperfoto *Cover*, 5, 7, 18b, 19, 25, 35, 36, 37, 44, 45; Science Museum/Science & Society Picture Library 17; Science Photo Library *Title page*, 9, 20, 21, 38, 41, 42; Getty Images 28, 43.

Illustrations by Nick Hawken and Tim Mayer

DID YOU KNOW ?

Most of the world's earthquakes occur around the edge of the Pacific Ocean – an area known as the 'Ring of Fire'.

▼ An elderly woman walks in a daze through the devastation caused by the Kobe earthquake, which hit Japan in January 1995, killing over 2,000 people.

Why study earthquakes?

Scientists throughout the world are carrying out research into improving ways of predicting earthquakes. At present, scientific predictions are often unreliable and severe earthquakes can happen without warning. Even if accurate predictions could be made, we would still be unable to stop an earthquake. However, we would be better prepared to put life-saving evacuation and rescue operations into action.

Long-term struggle

As well as killing people, a major earthquake destroys homes, shops, hospitals, roads, farmland, crops and livestock. Things we normally take for granted, such as clean water, food, shelter, gas, electricity and petrol, become a struggle to obtain. In addition, entire regions may need to be rebuilt, which can be very expensive and take months or even years.

Earthquake after-effects

Six main after-effects follow a major earthquake:

Loss of life

This is the worst effect. The majority of people who die are killed by collapsing buildings. However, if essential services such as hospitals are destroyed, deaths can continue for many days afterwards.

Shock and injury

People take a long time to recover from experiencing an earthquake. They may have been injured, seen their homes destroyed, and lost friends and relatives.

Buildings and sevices destroyed

Earthquakes can badly damage buildings. Tall tower blocks may collapse to the ground. Essential services, such as hospitals, fire stations and police stations, can be destroyed as well as homes.

Economy breakdown

With so much damage, the local economy (e.g. shops, banks, offices, factories) can break down, causing huge financial loss. The cost of rebuilding is usually very expensive.

More natural disasters

Earthquakes cause secondary after-effects which can cause as much destruction as the main shock. In addition to tsunamis (see p.32), they include landslides, mudslides and avalanches (see p.22).

Wildlife and farming

When natural areas such as woodland are destroyed, wild animals lose their habitats. Farmland and crops can also be destroyed.

66 EYEWITNESS 99

"My children were two steps behind me. They died in each other's arms and there was nothing I could do."

Catalina Valencia, Colombian earthquake survivor, 1999.

 **DID YOU KNOW ?**

The world's most powerful earthquake happened in Chile in 1960. It measured 9.3 on the Richter scale, which is over 100,000 more powerful than a nuclear explosion. The deadliest earthquake so far, in which 240,000 people died, occurred in Tangshan, China in 1976. The most expensive earthquake so far occurred in Kobe, Japan in 1995, causing major damage to roads and buildings.

▲ After this earthquake in Gibellina, Sicily, in January 1968, it took many months for people's lives to begin to return to normal.

This book looks at how earthquakes and tsunamis are caused and why they are so unpredictable and dangerous. It also explains how studying the earth and examining the evidence left by earthquakes helps scientists to discover new information and make more accurate predictions. Investigating the after-effects of earthquakes, looking at the precautions taken before a disaster and examining the rescue operations that followed teaches valuable life-saving lessons that can be used in the future.

EARTHQUAKE HORROR GIBELLINA, SICILY

Survivors are leaving stunned and homeless after the worst earthquake to hit Sicily for 60 years. Hundreds of homes have become piles of rubble and more than 300 are feared dead.

UPI report, 16 January 1968

What Causes Earthquakes?

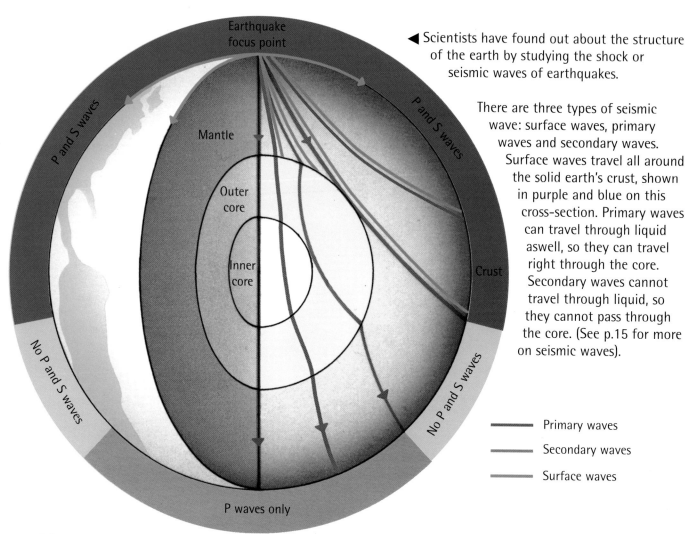

◄ Scientists have found out about the structure of the earth by studying the shock or seismic waves of earthquakes.

There are three types of seismic wave: surface waves, primary waves and secondary waves. Surface waves travel all around the solid earth's crust, shown in purple and blue on this cross-section. Primary waves can travel through liquid aswell, so they can travel right through the core. Secondary waves cannot travel through liquid, so they cannot pass through the core. (See p.15 for more on seismic waves).

——— Primary waves
——— Secondary waves
——— Surface waves

Labels in diagram: Earthquake focus point · P and S waves · P and S waves · Mantle · Outer core · Inner core · Crust · No P and S waves · No P and S waves · P waves only

Inside the earth

To understand how earthquakes are caused, it is important to understand the structure of our planet. Earth is made up of three main layers. The centre, or core, is the same size as the planet Mars and the temperature, at over 5,000 °C, is hotter than the surface of the sun! Surrounding the core lies the mantle, a thick layer of rock which is mainly solid, except close to the surface where it is molten (liquid). Floating on top of the mantle is the earth's thin outer layer, the crust. This is made up of separate slabs called tectonic plates. These huge plates are moved slowly around the planet by currents inside the mantle.

DID YOU KNOW ?

The earth is over 4,550 million years old and was first formed from a cloud of dust and gas.

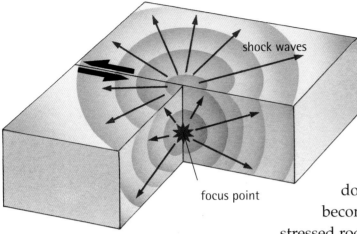

shock waves

focus point

Constant pressure

The solid rock of the crust is put under constant pressure from the movements of the plates. The plates are travelling in different directions at varying speeds and slide past each other with difficulty. In some places, one plate is slowly forced down underneath another. If moving rock becomes stuck, the pressure builds up until the stressed rocks suddenly tear apart, causing the violent ground movement we call an earthquake. The point where the rocks suddenly jolt or break is called the focus point. From here, powerful shock waves spread out in all directions.

▼ Folded rock strata in the cliff face of a road crossing the San Andreas fault. The twisting and folding is caused by immense stress on the rocks as the North American Plate slides past the Pacific Plate.

250 million years ago the land masses were joined in one huge continent.

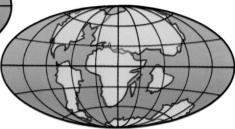

65 million years ago, the continents continued to move further apart.

130 million years ago, the continent started to split apart.

 ▲ The break-up of the supercontinent Pangaea took millions of years.

The restless continents

The earth's crust is separated into seven large and several smaller tectonic plates, which all fit together like a giant jigsaw puzzle. In 1915, German scientist Alfred Wegener introduced his theory of continental drift. He suggested that millions of years ago all the continents were joined together to form one supercontinent (which he named Pangaea, meaning 'all land'). Over millions of years, this supercontinent broke up and the pieces drifted to where they are situated now.

DID YOU KNOW ?

Wegener's theory of continental drift came from his discovery that the rocks and fossils of South America and South Africa were very similar. For many years his theory was doubted, but recent scientific research and studies of the ocean floor have added very strong evidence to support his ideas. Currently, continental drift is causing the Atlantic Ocean to expand while the Pacific Ocean is shrinking.

In 1965, scientist Sir Edward Bullard ▶ used one of the first computers to show how the coastlines of South America and Africa fit together.

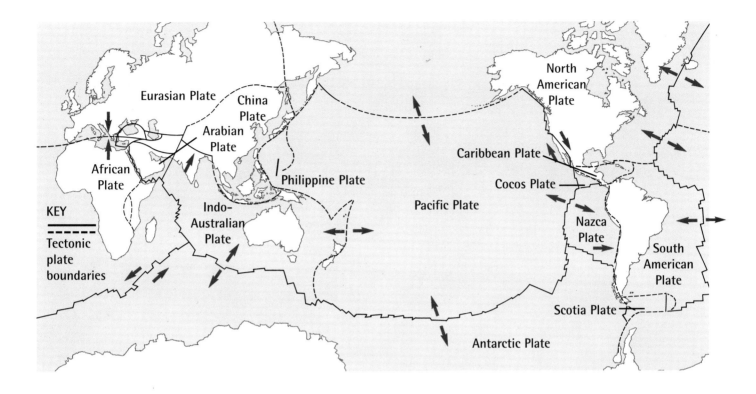

▲ This map shows the movement of the earth's tectonic plates. The pink arrows show the direction the plates are moving. It is along their boundaries that most earthquakes occur.

Today, the drift continues and the continents and oceans are still changing shape. Africa and North America are being pushed apart, while the Pacific Ocean is shrinking. Underneath the widening Atlantic Ocean, magma (molten rock) is flowing through from the mantle in places to form new ocean floor. The Mid-Atlantic ridge is a huge undersea mountain range beneath the Atlantic Ocean, which formed at one such spot where magma is constantly welling upwards.

DID YOU KNOW ?

The world's continents are moving at roughly the same rate as your fingernails are growing – about 2 cm per year.

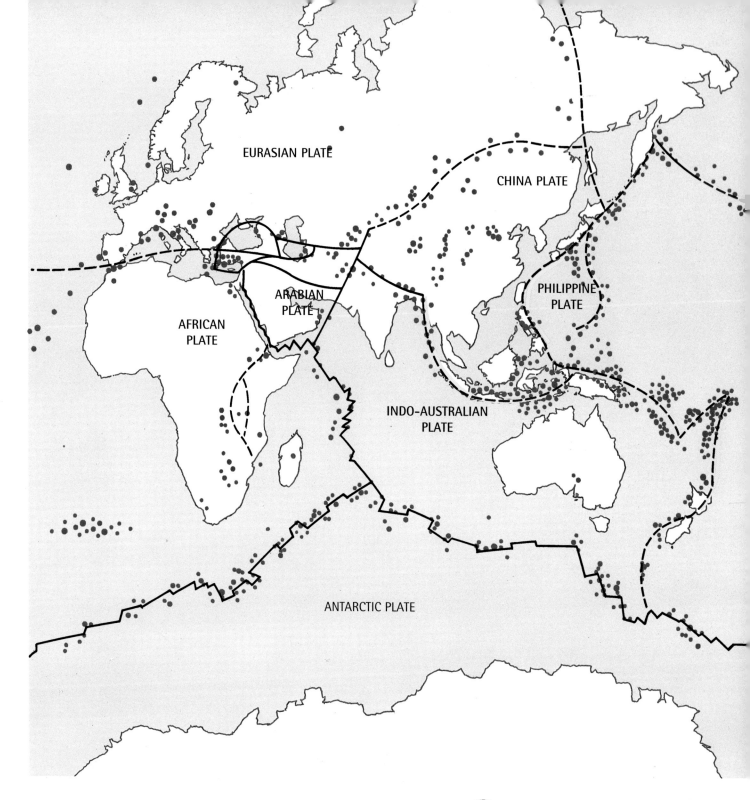

Subduction zones

Earthquakes occur at the boundaries or edges of plates which are grinding and scraping together. In some cases when plates collide, one plate is pushed down beneath the other in a process called subduction. Areas in the world where this happens are called subduction zones.

DID YOU KNOW ?

Earthquakes only occur in the crust. Deep earthquakes originate in crust that is sliding down beneath another tectonic plate.

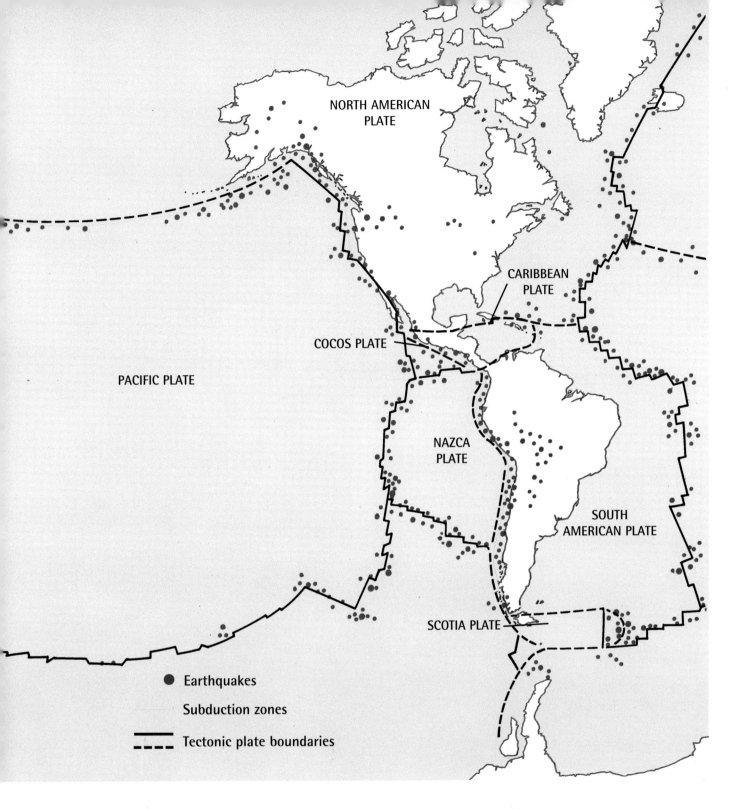

NORTH AMERICAN PLATE

CARIBBEAN PLATE

COCOS PLATE

PACIFIC PLATE

NAZCA PLATE

SOUTH AMERICAN PLATE

SCOTIA PLATE

- Earthquakes
- Subduction zones
- - - Tectonic plate boundaries

The 'Ring of Fire'

Subduction happens at three types of plate boundaries: ocean to ocean; ocean to continent; and continent to continent. The rim of the shrinking Pacific Ocean has the highest number of subduction zones. Earthquakes and volcanoes are extremely common here and it has been named the 'Ring of Fire'.

▲ The red dots on this map show the location of earthquakes around the world. You can see the many subduction zones that lie around the rim of the Pacific Plate, which scientists have called the 'Ring of Fire'.

Fault lines

The rocky surface of the crust is cut by millions of cracks or breaks called fault lines. They are the results of stress caused by the movement of molten rock in the mantle. If plates try to slide past each other along a fault line there is great friction between them and the solid rocks move with great difficulty. If you push two pieces of sandpaper together and then try to slide them apart smoothly, this will give you some idea of how hard it is for the rocks to move easily.

Friction build-up

The rocks on either side of the San Andreas fault in California, USA, do not move smoothly and often lock together. When this happens, tension and stress build up to a point where the rocks suddenly rip past each other to cause an earthquake.

Ground movement

The direction in which the land moves during an earthquake depends on which way the plates are travelling. The different types of faults below show that not only does the ground shake during an earthquake but large areas can move sideways and also up and down. In the 1964 Alaska earthquake, the ground level in some places dropped by over a metre.

▼ The type of fault line affects the direction the ground moves during an earthquake.

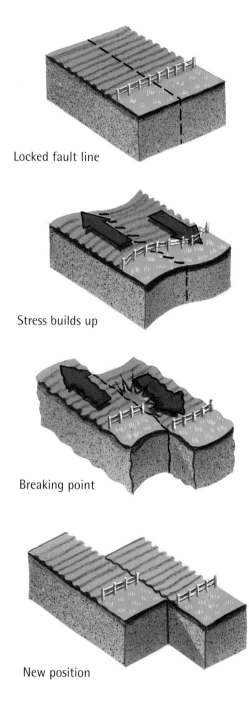

Locked fault line

Stress builds up

Breaking point

New position

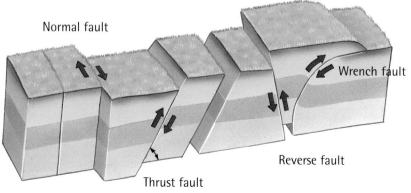

Normal fault

Wrench fault

Reverse fault

Thrust fault

Fractured rock layers

▲ It does not take a large amount of rock to get stuck for a sizeable earthquake to happen. If a 5-km section of rock along the San Andreas Fault line locks and then releases, it can cause an earthquake of magnitude 4.5 on the Richter scale.

Shock waves

The violent energy released during an earthquake produces three different types of energy waves. These pass through the rocks surrounding the epicentre (where the first shock reaches the earth's surface) and spread outwards, becoming steadily weaker.

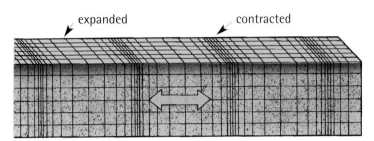

expanded   contracted

Primary waves

◄ The fastest waves are the primary waves, which travel at an average speed of 5 km per second. Primary waves cause the rocks to expand and contract like a spring being stretched and released.

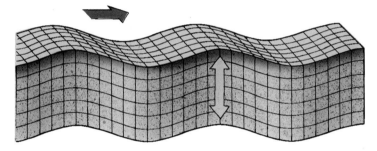

Secondary waves

◄ Secondary waves travel at an average speed of 3 km per second. They cannot travel through liquid, so they do not go into the earth's outer core. Secondary waves make rocks undulate up and down like ocean waves.

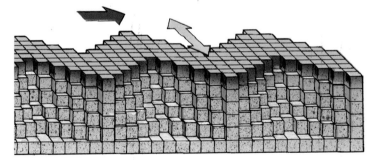

Surface waves move side to side.

◄ The slowest waves are the surface waves. During a shallow earthquake, it is the surface waves that carry most of the energy. The surface waves during the Chilean earthquake of 1960 were so powerful that they travelled twenty times around the earth and were still registering on seismometers after 60 hours.

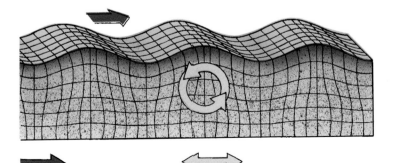

Surface waves move up and down.

Detecting and Measuring Earthquakes

Most shock waves transmitted by an earthquake are too small to be felt by human beings. However, they can be picked up by sensitive detection instruments called seismometers. A seismometer is placed below ground and records any vibrations digitally, just as on a CD. It is linked to a radio transmitter aerial which sends information to a central computer for analysis. At the receiving station, the seismologists (scientists who study earthquakes) identify any earthquake waves. As shock waves travel both round and through the planet, earthquakes can be monitored from anywhere in the world. Seismologists can use the international computer network to share important information immediately.

EARTHQUAKE INSTRUMENTS

A strainmeter measures changing pressures on rocks.

A borehole tiltmeter placed underground measures changes in ground level.

A long baseline tiltmeter measures changes in surface ground level.

A seismic truck sends shock waves into the ground to map rock layers.

Laser beams bounced between earth and an orbiting satellite measure rock movement.

Radio telescope signals are used to calculate rock movement.

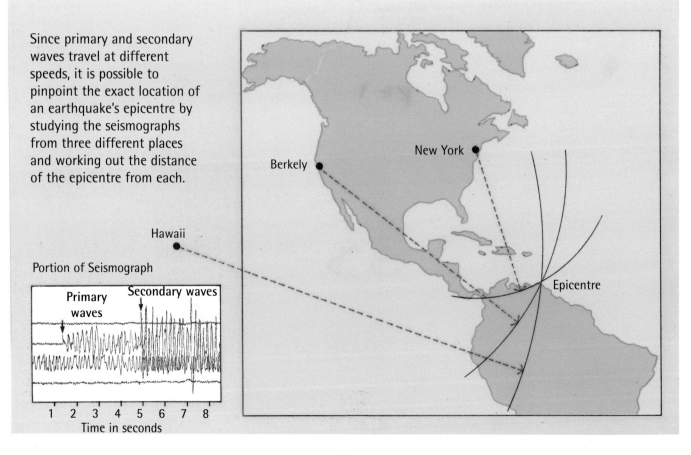

Since primary and secondary waves travel at different speeds, it is possible to pinpoint the exact location of an earthquake's epicentre by studying the seismographs from three different places and working out the distance of the epicentre from each.

New York

Berkely

Hawaii

Epicentre

Portion of Seismograph

Primary waves

Secondary waves

1 2 3 4 5 6 7 8

Time in seconds

Measuring earthquakes

Scientists grade earthquakes using two systems of measurement: magnitude and intensity. The Richter scale (magnitude) measures the size and strength of earthquakes, using numbers that range from magnitude 0–9. Each step up on the Richter scale is an increase of thirty times the amount of energy released by an earthquake. The Modified Mercalli Scale (intensity) grades earthquakes from I–XII (1–12) according to how damaging they are.

In about AD 130, Chinese philosopher Zhang Heng invented ▶ an instrument that recorded earthquakes and their direction. When the ground trembled, one or more of the eight dragon heads would drop a metal ball into the open mouth of a frog below.

Measuring earthquakes by magnitude and intensity

Magnitude	Intensity	Description
1.0–3.0	I	Not felt by people.
3.0–3.9	II–III	Felt by people at rest. Indoors, hanging objects may swing.
4.0–4.9	IV–V	Definite vibration felt; windows and objects rattle. Felt outdoors: liquid spills; doors swing.
5.0–5.9	VI–VII	Felt by everyone; difficult to stand; glass, china breaks; cracks appear in weak buildings; plaster and loose bricks fall; waves on ponds.
6.0–6.9	VIII–IX	Walls collapse; tall structures twist and fall; tree branches break. General panic: weak buildings shifted off foundations; underground pipes broken; cracks in ground; earthquake fountains.
7.0–	X–XII	Landslides; bridges destroyed; dams and embankments damaged. Few buildings survive; wide cracks in ground; railway tracks bent. Total destruction: objects thrown into the air; ground moves in waves.

Earthquake Hazards

When a large earthquake hits it is usually without warning and always with devastating results. The terrifying shaking of the ground lasts anything from a few seconds to a minute, as the stressed rocks along a fault line split apart and violently shift.

Scene of terror

The sudden ground movements from side to side and up and down cause incredible damage, especially in a town or city. Deep cracks can appear in roads or they can buckle upwards or collapse, crushing cars and drivers. Terrified people run into the streets to escape falling houses and are thrown to the ground. Shaking buildings break apart, and glass and bricks fly through the air. In addition, fuel and power lines are destroyed and there is the danger of fire breaking out.

▲ A rescue worker and her sniffer dog take a brief rest before they continue the gruelling job of searching for people trapped by the 1985 Mexican earthquake.

▲ Rescue workers dig out a victim alive after the 1995 Neftegorsk, Russia earthquake.

DID YOU KNOW ?

The most devasting earthquakes are those that are strong, shallow (with the focus point less than 30 km underground) and occur in highly populated areas.

Powerless

As the ground stops shaking, the air is filled with the sounds of sirens and screams. There is no electricity, so telephones and life-saving equipment are useless. The rescuers are faced with a nightmare: their first priority is to find the survivors, give emergency medical treatment and then transport the injured to the nearest hospital. The journey will be perilous as aftershocks are likely to affect the roads.

Rescue

Some survivors are trapped beneath piles of rubble. Sniffer dogs and infra-red cameras are used to try and locate anyone alive. Everyone knows that it is a race against time to free them, in case aftershocks occur, or a build-up of gas fumes causes an explosion.

▼ The Kobe earthquake in western Japan was so violent that it caused the Hanshin highway to collapse.

Taking Action

Anyone who is indoors when an earthquake strikes should either crouch in the doorway (the strongest part of a building) or get down on the floor under a sturdy desk or table.

The residents of Parkfield, California in the USA, live on top of the San Andreas fault system (see p. 28). They are used to earthquakes and know exactly what to do if one strikes. In Parkfield School, the children regularly practise their earthquake drill. At a signal from their teacher, they crouch under their desks and cover their heads with their arms. The desks are bolted to the floor, all computers and heavy equipment are also firmly bolted down and the windows are criss-crossed with tape to prevent broken glass flying through the air.

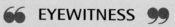 ▲ Children practising their earthquake drill in Parkfield, California, USA.

66 EYEWITNESS 99

"When the earth started shaking I thought it must be the end of the world. I could feel myself falling ... The bedroom ceiling fell down on me."

Earthquake survivor, Golcuk, Turkey, 1999

Normal building   Earthquake-proof building

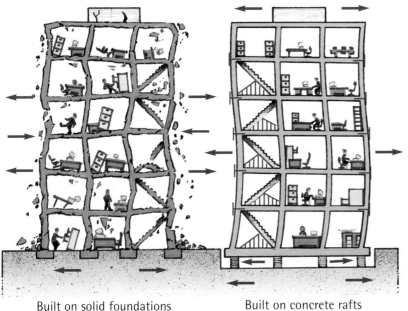

Built on solid foundations with no reinforcements.

Built on concrete rafts and reinforced.

HIGH-RISE RISK

Most people who die in earthquakes are killed by collapsing buildings. Very tall buildings are most at risk. Not only do they sway but they also twist, putting great pressure on the materials from which they are built. In highly populated cities, tall buildings are often situated close together. During strong earthquakes, swaying tower blocks have sometimes battered buildings around them until they have collapsed.

▲ Earthquake-proof buildings float on concrete rafts so that when they shake, the whole building sways and stays in one piece.

Precautions

In many cities situated in an earthquake zone, contractors must follow strict rules when repairing damaged buildings or constructing new ones. The walls, floors, roofs and foundations of buildings must be strengthened to withstand shock waves. Specially treated materials and building methods are used to construct earthquake-proof buildings. Flexible, unbreakable power lines are even used in some cities. However, these precautions are expensive and often impossible to carry out in poorer countries.

▲ Buildings in the Marina district of San Francisco collapsed during the Loma Prieta 1989 earthquake as they were built on an old landfill site.

Avalanches and Landslides

Earthquakes can cause landslides and avalanches in mountainous regions.

Avalanches

In May 1970, an undersea earthquake measuring 7.7 on the Richter scale caused the overhanging north face of the Huascarán mountain, Peru, to collapse in an avalanche of snow and rock. Eyewitnesses said they had heard a sonic boom (explosive sound) at the same time as they felt the earthquake's tremors. There was a strong blast of air, after which the avalanche of snow and rock fell over 4,000 m into the Rio Santo valley.

▲ The deadly path of the Peruvian avalanche seen from the air.

The avalanche turned into a heaving stream of mud, ice and boulders, flowing at about 280 kph. The flow made the ground shake as it passed and boulders flew through the air at speeds of up to 1,000 kph. Within six minutes the town of Yungay had been wiped out, buried under 10 m of rock debris. More than 50,000 people were killed by the avalanche.

 DID YOU KNOW ?

Earthquakes can be caused by people. Mining, dam-building and oil and gas extraction all put stress on underground rocks, which can cause a tremor.

THE PATH OF DEATH IN PERU

Two avalanches wiped out the town of Yungay after the earthquake in Peru on 31 May, 1970. The avalanche descended upon the town from the Cordillera Blanca, one of two mountain ranges running north-west to south-east. Helicopter pilots estimated that 2,500 people took refuge on Yungay Cemetery Hill before the town was overwhelmed. Those who survived on the hill were safe but unable to escape in any direction.

Press Association report, 8 June 1970

Landslides

In 1959, Madison Canyon in Montana, USA, was devastated by a landslide that followed a 7.1 magnitude earthquake. The landslide swamped a camp site, killing 19 people. It also dammed streams, which caused widespread flooding. Shock waves from the earthquake had also damaged the Hebgen Dam, putting the people living downstream in serious danger. Before the dam could be repaired and the flooded areas drained, heavy earth-moving machinery had to be brought in to dig a channel through the debris. The earthquake that had caused such damaging after-effects had been so powerful that it had also altered the timing between geyser eruptions at nearby Yellowstone Park and caused changes in ground level measuring up to 6 m.

RELIEF OPERATION UNDERWAY

Relief operations are gathering momentum in the remote region of northern India which was hit by a severe earthquake in the early hours of Monday. Hundreds of road workers have been sent in to clear landslide debris from a 16km stretch of road leading to the worst-affected area. "It looks like half the mountain has come off," said Chamoli district magistrate Uma Kant Pawar.

Online news report, BBC, 30 March 1999

Mudslides

The effects of shock waves on soft, wet ground can be dramatic. The soil particles are so loosely packed together that they easily separate. When water mixes in, the soil turns to thick mud and the previously solid ground collapses. Houses built on soft ground, such as old landfill sites or reclaimed marshland, are no longer supported and fall over or sink. This was a major after-effect of the Mexico City earthquake in 1985. However, in many high-risk earthquake zones, strict building laws are in place to stop this happening.

▲ 27 March 1964: A house uprooted by a landslide in Anchorage, Alaska.

Earthquake Disasters

Japan

The island of Japan is situated in the Pacific Ocean on a very unstable part of the earth's crust. It lies on a subduction zone where two plates are diving down beneath a third.

The Great Kanto Earthquake

The Great Kanto Earthquake struck Japan on 1 September 1923. The focus point of this massive undersea earthquake was located off the coast of Yokohama, 80 km from Tokyo. The earthquake measured 8.3 on the Richter scale and was so powerful that a split appeared in the sea floor. Thousands of buildings in Tokyo were destroyed and 100,000 people were killed. A tsunami followed almost immediately, causing more destruction.

Fire

When the earthquake struck, many people were cooking their midday meal on open stoves. The wood and paper houses caught fire easily and a terrifying fire storm spread rapidly through the city. Damaged gas and electricity supplies also sparked off fires. People who managed to escape the burning flames suffocated through lack of oxygen.

The next day, another strong tremor struck, causing more devastation. Smaller aftershocks then followed.

▲ Villagers in Japan look through the wreckage caused by the Great Kanto earthquake of 1923.

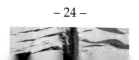

▲ After the devastation of an earthquake, clean drinking water is a scarce essential.

EARTHQUAKE DEATHS FALL

"The average number of deaths from earthquakes over the last 18 years has come down to about 8,000 a year. That reduction is probably due to countries making buildings safer."

Dr. Waverley Person, Director, National Earthquake Information Center, USA.

▼ This map shows the site of the Great Kanto earthquake and its epicentre.

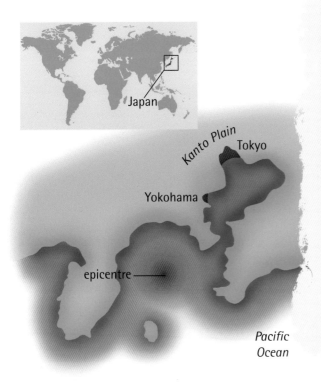

Japan

Kanto Plain

Tokyo

Yokohama

epicentre ———

Pacific Ocean

Lessons learned

From the Great Kanto and other earthquakes, the Japanese learned some valuable lessons. Nowadays, cities such as Tokyo have strict building laws and disaster teams ready for action. Many inhabitants have emergency supply kits, prepared with food, water and medicine and take part in earthquake drills. In October 1994, an earthquake of magnitude 7.9 happened in the ocean crust off Hokkaido, the most northern Japanese island, causing many buildings to collapse. Three months later a 6.9 earthquake shattered the city of Kobe. The earthquake precautions saved lives and although 5,000 people died, the number of deaths could have been far higher.

▲ Locals and soldiers together desperately try to rescue trapped people after the Armenian earthquake, using their bare hands because of the lack of proper equipment.

Armenia

On 7 December 1988, an earthquake of magnitude 6.9 struck at the southern end of the Lesser Caucasus Mountains in Armenia. Although large tremors had been felt before in the area, no large earthquake had ever been recorded there. No earthquake precautions had ever been taken either. It is thought that the number of people who died as a result of the earthquake is between 25,000 to 100,000.

Collapsed buildings

The damage to buildings in Armenia was huge. In the town of Leninakan, where 290,000 people lived, 80 per cent of the buildings collapsed. In Spitak (population 20,000) all buildings were damaged. The worst damage happened in an area of Spitak where tower blocks had been built on former marshland. The strength of the earthquake tremors collapsed the weakened ground.

In this mountainous region, no precautions had been taken to strengthen buildings against the possibility of earthquakes or landslides. Many buildings were prefabricated (ready-made in sections) from concrete slabs and during the earthquake the sections had simply fallen apart. A number of factories were badly damaged but, incredibly, the two local nuclear reactors were not affected.

HIGH COST OF SAFETY

"More and more people are being concentrated in urban areas, which makes the effects of any earthquake much worse, and some countries find it hard to afford the cost of making houses safe."

Dr. Waverley Person, Director of National Earthquakes Information Center, USA.

Armenia —▫

ARMENIA

Caspian Sea

Black Sea

Spitak

Leninakan

Lake Sevan

 Recorded earthquake damage zone

◀ This map shows the site of the Armenia earthquake of 1988.

Lessons learned

The key lesson learned in Armenia was never to give up searching for survivors. Another lesson was that the poor building methods used in the area meant more search and rescue teams and equipment should have been sent in. The speed of rescue operations was also important: many trapped people suffocated, or died from their injuries or the cold. The local hospitals were out of action and injured people had to be transported long distances along poor roads for treatment.

ARMENIAN EARTHQUAKE TRAGEDY

Every spare hand carries out the frantic clear-up operation – life and death for the victims trapped beneath the debris. Some say lack of proper communication and central organisation hampered this concerted search effort.

Camera Press/TASS press agencies report, December 1988

Search and rescue

Immediately after the disaster, search and rescue missions were organized by local people. Specialist volunteers and the sixteen international aid teams did not arrive for another two days. The major after-effect of this earthquake was the huge number of collapsed buildings and the numbers of people trapped under them. Many of the older buildings survived because they had been built from much stronger local rock. The main work of the rescue operation was finished ten days after the earthquake had struck. Amazingly, survivors were being found up to nine days later.

▲ Many people died in earthquake damaged buildings.

66 EYEWITNESS 99

"I heard a deep rumbling sound that was just a couple of seconds before the shock hit. The ground was heaving and shaking. I could hear Katy screaming. I could hear crockery breaking, windows breaking, the chimney ripping through the roof."

Kathy Mathew, Lomo Prieta, California 1989

California

The state of California, USA, lies along the boundary between two tectonic plates. Most of California lies on top of the slow-moving North American plate which is travelling southwards. The rest is carried by the Pacific plate which is grinding past it much faster in a northwest direction. As a result, a pattern of fault-lines covers the state, any of which could produce an earthquake. Each year, earthquake instruments detect more than 20,000 tremors. The most famous fault is the visible San Andreas fault which stretches through the state for over 1,100 km. In 1999, seismologists discovered a previously unknown fault lying deep under the city of Los Angeles. Named the Puente Hills fault, they believe it could produce an earthquake bigger than any yet to have hit southern California.

▲ The visible San Andreas fault cuts across California. A major earthquake could hit California at any time. Movement along the San Andreas fault system could cause massive destruction in cities from Los Angeles (population 3.5 million people) to San Francisco (population 750,000 people).

The 1906 earthquake

By 1906, California had changed from an underpopulated area to a rapidly developing state. The effects of the huge earthquake that hit San Francisco on 18 April 1906 were devastating. It measured 8.3 on the Richter scale and caused the ground to shift along more than 400 km of the San Andreas fault. Although the shaking lasted for less than a minute it was felt as far away as Oregon. Witnesses saw the ground heave up and down, trees snap in two, eruptions of sand fountains, and landslips. Most houses were made of wood and so survived the shock, but hundreds of buildings were destroyed by a fire that raged through the city. About 300,000 people were made homeless and emergency centres were set up to help them.

▼ This map shows the site of the San Francisco earthquake of 1906.

Lessons learned

The main lessons learned from the San Francisco earthquake were about building methods. Buildings constructed on top of solid rock survived better than those on soft ground. Wooden buildings also survived better than those built of brick or stone. One of the most important outcomes was that the geologist H. F. Reid collected enough information to put forward the first modern explanation of earthquakes together with ideas for predicting them.

California

• San Francisco

Pacific Ocean

Recorded earthquake damage zone

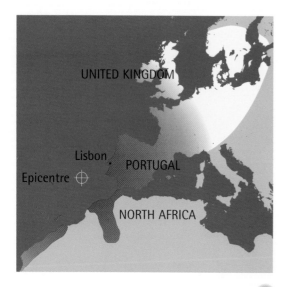

Other Famous Earthquakes

◄ 1755 Lisbon, Portugal (8.7)

This massive undersea earthquake killed more than 25,000 in Lisbon. Damage to buildings and a firestorm added to the destruction. The earthquake caused a tsunami that was felt in Britain and in the Caribbean, 4,500 km away. Tremors damaged the north African coast, which made people think there had been two earthquakes. This was the first earthquake to be studied by scientists.

Recorded earthquake damage zone

1857 Naples, Italy (6.5) ►

This earthquake killed 12,000. An engineer, Robert Mallet, set out to study the earthquake's effects and his was one of the first systematic and painstaking investigations based on observation and measurement. Not only did he work out that the earthquake had erupted from a single focus point, with shock waves passing through the ground, but also that the severe damage could be blamed on poor building techniques.

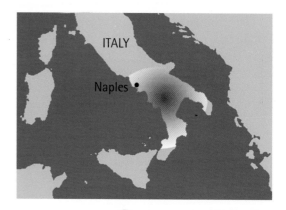

Earthquake damage zone

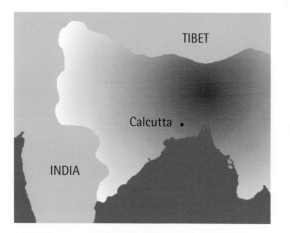

◄ 1897 Assam, India (8.7)

Scientists used seismic instruments to study the Assam earthquake and their discoveries confirmed the existence of three types of earthquake waves.

Earthquake damage zone

1960 Santiago, Chile (9.3) ►

The most powerful recorded earthquake, which killed more than 5,000 people. The surface shock waves were so strong that they were still being recorded on seismographs 60 hours later.

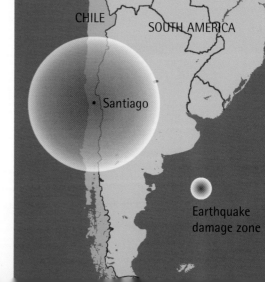

Earthquake damage zone

◄ 1964 Alaska, USA (8.3-8.6)

The focus point of this undersea earthquake was about 129 km east of Anchorage, Alaska. The city was badly damaged and hundreds lost their homes. The shape of the coastline was altered by powerful surface waves. The earthquake also caused a huge tsunami which was recorded in Antarctica.

Earthquake damage zone

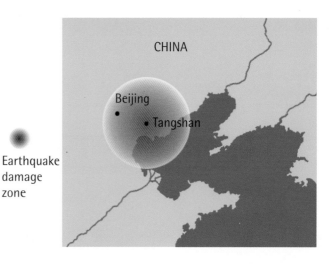

1976 Tangshan, China (7.5) ►

This was China's most damaging earthquake for 400 years. The intense shaking of the main shock lasted for just over twenty seconds but was followed over the next two days by 125 smaller aftershocks. More than 240,000 people were killed.

Earthquake damage zone

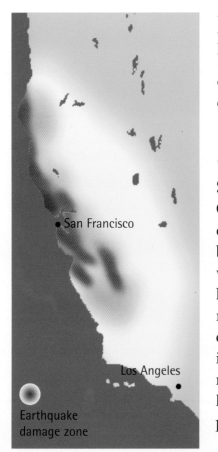

Earthquake damage zone

◄ 1989 Loma Prieta, California USA (7.1)

Movement along the San Andreas fault line caused this earthquake. Damage in the San Francisco area was mainly to buildings constructed on poor ground. Another unseen after-effect was that elevated (two-tier) roads collapsed.

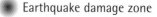

Earthquake damage zone

1999 Armenia, Colombia, ► South America (6.3)

Over 2,000 people died in this earthquake, mostly from collapsing buildings. Half the town of Armenia was flattened, leaving over 180,000 homeless. Many died because local rescue teams lacked equipment and experience, and it took two days for international teams to arrive. The region's poverty means that it will be a long time before it is rebuilt and productive.

Tsunamis

An earthquake that occurs under the ocean can be just as destructive as one on land. The shifting of the ocean floor can cause a giant wave called a tsunami to form. A tsunami is not like a normal sea wave. It is a powerful energy wave that stretches in a column of water from the sea-floor to the surface. Because it contains so much energy, a tsunami can race across the ocean for thousands of kilometres at speeds of up to 900 kph. The wave height of a tsunami is in proportion to the depth of water it is travelling across. So, in the middle of the ocean a tsunami surface wave is very small and ships can pass over it without noticing. Once the tsunami gets closer to land, it becomes a giant wave up to 30 m high, which slams into the coast. The highest point of a tsunami is called its peak wave.

DID YOU KNOW ?

The Chilean earthquake of 1960 caused a tsunami which 22 hours later hit the coast of Japan 17,000 km away, causing the deaths of 200 people.

▼ An underwater earthquake sends an energy wave racing across the ocean. The height of the surface waves (h) increases as the ocean depth (d) decreases. Some tsunamis can be as high as 30 m when they hit the coast.

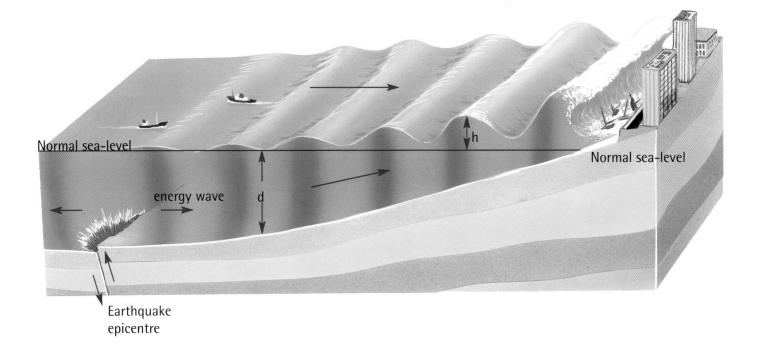

Normal sea-level

Normal sea-level

energy wave

d

h

Earthquake epicentre

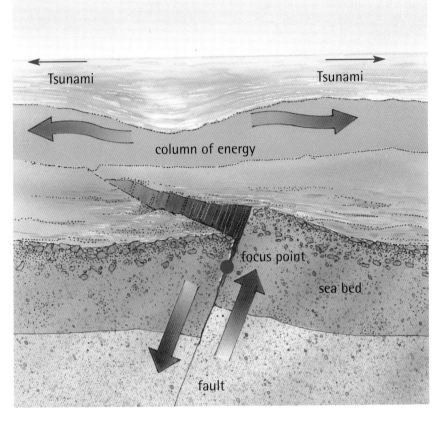

The violent movement of the sea bed during an earthquake sends an energy wave into the ocean that starts a tsunami.

Pacific peril

Nearly all dangerous tsunamis occur in the Pacific Ocean because it is surrounded by moving tectonic plates (see pages 12-13). Tsunami damage costs the USA more than £30 million in damage to property each year. In addition, 500,000 people in the USA live in areas at risk from tsunamis of up to 15 m in height and 1.2 million are at risk from a 30-m wave. A big tsunami can sweep across the Pacific Ocean in about 24 hours. Most devastation occurs within 400 km of its starting point. Inside this 400 km, the wave will hit coastlines in less than 30 minutes, leaving very little time to alert local authorities and to start evacuating an area.

In 1755, a huge killer wave smashed into the city of Lisbon.

During the twentieth century, 43 minor tsunamis occurred in the Mediterranean area. Only two big tsunamis are known to have hit Europe. In 1530 BC, a tsunami destroyed towns on the island of Crete and battered Mediterranean coasts. In 1755, an earthquake in the eastern Atlantic Ocean caused a tsunami that killed 25,000 people in Lisbon, Portugal, and was felt as far away as Scotland and the Caribbean.

Papua New Guinea

Papua New Guinea

On 17 July 1998, a tsunami hit the town of Sandaun in Papua New Guinea, an island north-east of Australia. It caused over 2,500 fatalities, the largest number of deaths caused by a tsunami this century. The International Tsunami Survey Team (ITST) arrived two weeks after the disaster to survey the damage and to work out what had happened. The earthquake epicentre was pinpointed at a distance of 50 km away from the coastline. Working from the speed a tsunami travels, this meant the villages were hit less than four minutes after feeling the first tremor. There had been no time to evacuate anyone, even with an excellent early warning system. The worst damage and highest waves (up to 15 m) happened along a 30 km stretch of coast between two villages.

DISASTER TIDAL WAVE – SIMMANO, PAPUA NEW GUINEA

First reports coming through from Papua New Guinea state that rescue workers believe that up to 3,000 people were swept to their deaths when three giant tidal waves struck on 17 July and devastated seven coastal towns.

AFP press agency, July 1998

Landslide

The earthquake measured 7.7 on the Richter scale, which is not strong enough on its own to have caused a tsunami with a peak wave 15 m above land! However, researchers discovered that the earthquake had also caused an undersea landslide. This catastrophic ground movement had increased the energy and height of the tsunami.

◀ The powerful wave that battered Papua New Guinea towered above houses and swept over a kilometre inland.

DID YOU KNOW?

Tsunamis are known as killer waves for these three reasons:

1. The wave's impact is strong enough to kill people and seriously damage buildings.
2. The wave can pick up and suck in objects.
3. Anything swept up into the wave smashes against other objects.

▼ Gerry Monana holds a kitten that she has rescued. Behind her is all that is left of her village after the 15-m-high tsunami hit Papua New Guinea in 1998.

Relief and Rescue

After an earthquake, the authorities must decide on a plan of action. Once the initial damage has been assessed, the top priority is to organize the rescue of people trapped under collapsed buildings. There is no time to waste – within two to six hours, only half the number of people trapped will still be alive.

International rescue

It is for this reason that international rescue teams, such as the IRC (International Rescue Corps) were formed, to respond instantly to emergencies worldwide. The IRC was set up in Britain in 1980, after an earthquake hit southern Italy killing 3,000 people. The IRC carries medicine, relief supplies, radio equipment, infra-red cameras (which find people by locating their body heat) and sniffer dogs. Volunteers are on standby 24 hours a day and work closely with governments, the United Nations, the Red Cross and other relief organizations.

1. Assess damage.

2. Rescue people trapped under buildings.

3. Provide emergency medical assistance area.

4. Assess survivors' needs for food, water and shelter.

5. Provide emergency aid.

6. Assess damage to buildings. Demolish dangerous buildings.

7. Restore communications and economic activity.

8. Start rebuilding. Start programme of earthquake education.

▲ This is the ideal relief and rescue sequence that should follow an earthquake.

Sniffer dogs can quickly ▶ smell the scent of people trapped inside collapsed buildings.

▲ A rescue worker comforts a woman as others work on freeing her leg from rubble, after an earthquake in Neftegorsk, Russia, in May 1995.

Medical treatment

People pulled out alive from under the rubble of collapsed buildings need medical attention. However, since medical resources are usually limited, a special emergency system, called Triage, is used. Triage is used to work out which survivors would gain the most from immediate medical help, and which can wait to be seen by a doctor. It is a similar system to that used in hospital casualty units, except casualties who are near death and who cannot be saved, are not treated. All rescue workers have some medical training and carry basic life-saving equipment with them. If hospitals are out of action, the injured are taken to temporary medical centres for treatment.

66 EYEWITNESS 99

"We don't have enough needles, antibiotics, basic medicines. We have no ventilators. People should bring anything they can, even toilet paper, with them. If we don't receive immediate help, we simply won't be able to cope."

Gloria Cardenas, nurse, Colombia, January 1999

TENTS AND PRAYER

The aid workers knew they had a massive disaster on their hands. An earthquake (last week) had killed as many as 5,000 people and wreaked havoc on 95 villages in northern Afghanistan. Thousands of survivors needed help – and the international rescuers couldn't do a thing about it. They had fleets of experienced workers with satellite phones, stretchers and medical supplies. They had food – 700 tonnes of it. But they didn't have decent weather. Rain and hail poured down on the airstrip, keeping planes and helicopters from making it to the disaster area and back. "It's basically a problem of logistics, not of money," said UN spokesman Rupert Colville.

Extract from a report in *Newsweek* magazine, 15 June 1998

Longer term relief

Despite the efforts of the rescue teams, the effects of an earthquake continue long after it first strikes. Studies have shown that the majority of deaths from an earthquake or tsunami happen within the first two days. However disease, which can often kill as many as the earthquake itself, comes later.

Disease

This second phase of deaths usually starts about four days after the disaster. The authorities must take steps to prevent disease spreading, such as making sure water supplies stay clean. In this way, the number of deaths can be dramatically reduced. In the aftermath of the Papua New Guinea tsunami of 1998, it was essential to find and bury as many dead bodies as possible. Otherwise, corpses may have contaminated drinking water and caused many fatal diseases.

Shelter

The next priority is to get people sheltered and re-housed. In the case of the Colombian earthquake in January 1999, over 200,000 people in Armenia were made homeless. Emergency housing after an earthquake or tsunami can be in hotels, mobile trailers, holiday homes, schools, offices and even on ships, trains and buses. Tents have been used as temporary homes after earthquakes for many years and shelters can even be constructed from easily transported plastic sheeting to give short-term protection.

◀ After the Mexico earthquake of 1985, even the rubble from collapsed buildings was used for temporary housing.

DID YOU KNOW ?

Many foreign governments give large sums of money when disaster strikes another nation. Within days of being struck by the devastating earthquake in January 1999, more than $3 million dollars in foreign aid had been pledged to help Colombia's recovery.

▼ After the Armenian earthquake in the Russian Federation, Italian builders helped create a whole town from temporary buildings. The town included shops, schools and clinics.

Temporary buildings

In countries that can afford it, temporary prefabricated buildings are a good solution to the desperate need for housing. A building of 40 square m can be easily transported on a flat-bed truck. In addition, prefabricated buildings can be connected to electricity, gas, water and sewerage lines.

Redevelopment

A devastated area must be rebuilt as quickly as possible. Poorer countries may have extra problems: although international aid contributes towards redevelopment, the stricken country may sometimes pay up to 80 per cent of the cost. For this reason, emergency housing in developing countries must be cheap and simple. After earthquakes in Peru and Nicaragua, the relief agencies invented a building method called 'stack-sack'. Houses were built using sandbags filled with cement-mix and further strengthened with steel reinforced bars.

Predicting Earthquakes

Predicting earthquakes is extremely difficult, but it is possible. In 1975, the evacuation was ordered of three large cities in the Haicheng-Yingkou area of China: 48 hours later an earthquake of magnitude 7.3 struck. Although it destroyed 50 square km of homes, only 1,300 people died and 16,000 were injured – an exceptionally low number for such a large earthquake.

Natural warning signs

Scientists worldwide are investigating the most reliable methods of predicting earthquakes. Some scientists are also investigating less reliable natural warning signs. These include 'earthquake lights' – bolts of electricity in the air produced by stressed rocks – and strange animal behaviour. High-frequency noise from stressed rocks or changes in their magnetic field may warn animals to desert an area, or wake from hibernation before an earthquake.

Safety on the Bullet Train

In many earthquake zones, alarms are used. For one of the fastest trains in the world, such a warning system is essential. Japan's Bullet Train travels at 240 kph and carries over 340,000 passengers a day. Its alarm system directly links seismic stations built every 20 km along the railway lines. If significant ground movement is detected, the power to the railway lines is shut off. The train takes about 70 seconds to stop over a distance of 2.5 km. This is quick enough for the train to stop before the earthquake hits the line.

▲ The Japanese Bullet Train is one of the fastest trains in the world.

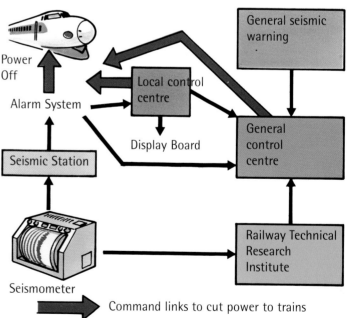

Bullet train

Power Off

Alarm System

General seismic warning

Local control centre

Display Board

Seismic Station

General control centre

Seismometer

Railway Technical Research Institute

Command links to cut power to trains

▲ This diagram shows the complex alarm system which ensures power to the Bullet Train is shut off as soon as earthquake waves are detected.

PREDICTION METHODS

Scientists in earthquake zones look for these changes in the earth's structure which could be warning signs of a major earthquake:

1. Changes in the speed of waves travelling through rock

Before a major earthquake rocks are under increased stress, causing the energy levels of the P and S waves to change.

2. Ground tilt

Tiltmeters and extensionmeters are instruments that measure small changes in the ground, such as rising or sinking. As stress causes the ground to buckle this can be detected long before a big earthquake.

3. Rock gases

Small ground tremors and stress cause new cracks to open up in rocks. Underground water seeps into the cracks and dissolves more of the rock gases, such as radon. Scientists can detect this increase by analyzing the water as it comes to the surface.

4. The tides

Before a big earthquake, rocks may change position. When these movements are underwater, e.g. along a coastline, the height of the tides can be altered.

5. Changes in electrical and magnetic properties of rocks

The great stress the rocks are under changes their electrical and magnetic properties.

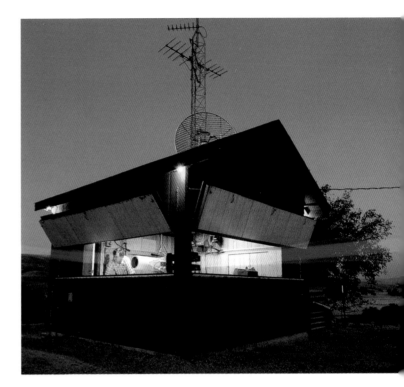

▲ Scientists at Parkfield, California, USA use the latest technology in their earthquake prediction programme. Here, scientists carry out an experiment using lasers that monitor minute ground movements.

66 EYEWITNESS 99

"About ten days before the Kobe earthquake, while having an evening piano lesson I looked up at the clock – the hand suddenly dropped down. There were other things. The air conditioner worked on its own without the remote control switch. The day before the earthquake, the moon looked very pink that evening. Back at the house, the TV channels kept switching of their own accord."

Hatsumi Haryama, Kobe, Japan, 1995

Using computers

Getting people out of high-rise buildings during and after an earthquake is difficult and dangerous. Investigators have found from studying previous earthquakes that people are in shock and can only remember simple, direct instructions. A computer simulation of the different escape routes is used to design the simplest and safest ways of evacuating people. Computer simulations are also used to work out the best methods for rescuing injured people from a damaged tall building.

Earthquake-proof

Architects use computer simulation to design buildings that can withstand an earthquake (see p.21). The Transamerica Building in San Francisco, California was designed by computer and rigorously tested using computer simulation before it was built.

▼ The Transamerica Building in San Francisco, which was designed and built to withstand major earthquakes.

DID YOU KNOW ?

The insurance costs of an earthquake are huge and not just because of the devastation. Claims are also made for loss of earnings, loss of information from destroyed computers, long-term injuries, loss of valuable works of art and damage to historic buildings.

Safety response

Because earthquakes can be so unpredictable and the results so devastating, the United Nations have suggested safety measures to be taken by national and local governments, companies and the local people. If these safety measures are taken once an earthquake prediction has been made, then damage and deaths caused by the earthquake can be greatly lessened.

Detailed work is being done ▶ to understand how we can make earthquake-damaged buildings safer in the future.

▼ The United Nations has suggested this safety plan to help countries prepare for and cope with earthquakes.

	TIME AFTER EARTHQUAKE		
	Up to 2 days	2 to 4 months	Up to 12 months
Protection of human life	Equip the danger area; prepare emergency medical centres	Continue emergency measures and rebuild medical centres	Plan emergency food stores; plan the role of medical centres
Special measures	Cut off electricity and gas mains; shut down nuclear reactors and dangerous chemical plants.	Remove or safeguard hazardous substances; lower water reservoir levels, etc.	Transfer hazardous substances to safe storage
Buildings	Evacuate dangerous buildings; close public buildings	Estimate probable damages; prepare evacuation plans	Strengthen vulnerable buildings

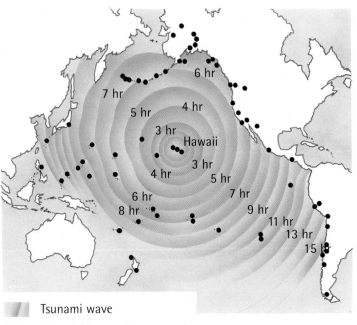

Tsunami wave

• Seismic/tide stations

▲ This map shows the tsunami early warning system and the time it takes a tsunami to travel across the Pacific Ocean.

Tsunami early warning

An early warning system for tsunamis is provided for all the Pacific nations. The Pacific Tsunami Warning System includes 23 nations and has 69 seismic stations and 65 tide stations. Any earthquake greater than 6.5 on the Richter scale will set off an alarm, while an earthquake above 7.5 will result in a round-the-clock tsunami watch. An official tsunami warning will only be given if it is certain that a wave has been created, and only then for areas at least an hour's distance from the earthquake epicentre.

Precautions

Safety measures for tsunamis include the following:
- Planning evacuation drills, including escape routes to high ground.
- Putting public education programmes into action.
- Building housing on high ground, away from danger zones.
- Constructing offshore breakwaters to weaken the impact of a tsunami.
- Strengthening buildings to stand up to the full force of the wave.

TSUNAMI WARNING

On 16 August at 10.27 GMT or 8.27 pm local time an earthquake with a magnitude of 7.8 on the open-ended Richter scale occurred in the Pacific Ocean off the coasts of Bougainville, New Britain and New Ireland. A tsunami watch and warning has been issued for the western Pacific Ocean.

Emergency Information Administrator, Disaster Information Center, 17 August 1995

◄ This is the scene of devastation that greeted the International Tsunami Survey Team in Papua New Guinea in 1998.

▲ A young girl with protective head padding hides under her desk as part of a regular Japanese school earthquake drill.

Earthquakes are natural disasters and it is impossible to prevent them from occurring. Scientific research into predicting when and where they will happen continues to advance, but methods are still not 100 per cent reliable. However, action can be taken to limit the damage and loss of life they can cause by having public education programmes, building control regulations and international rescue teams to make vulnerable areas safer.

Glossary

Aftershock Weaker shock that follows the main shock of an earthquake.

Avalanche Mass of snow, ice or rock that breaks away from a mountainside and slides down a steep slope.

Continental drift The theory that the continents can move around the earth's surface.

Continental plate Tectonic plate made up of land.

Core The region at the centre of the earth which has a solid inner part and a liquid outer part.

Crust The thin outer layer of the earth, also called the lithosphere.

Developing country A poor country that is trying to improve its economy.

Epicentre Point on the earth's surface directly above an earthquake's focus point.

Fault line Crack or break in the earth's crust.

Focus point Starting point of an earthquake, where the stress is released when rocks suddenly move or break.

Intensity Amount of damage caused by an earthquake.

Landslide Mass of rock and soil that suddenly breaks away from a hillside or mountain.

Tectonic plate One of the slabs of the earth's crust (lithosphere).

Liquefaction Shaking soil particles and water so much during an earthquake that solid ground turns into liquid mud.

Magma Molten or liquid rock in the mantle and outer core of the earth

Mantle The layer of rock between the earth's crust and the core where magma originates.

Mid-Atlantic ridge Undersea mountain range formed by magma flowing up through the crust, which is pushing the tectonic plates apart.

Modified Mercalli scale A scale that measures earthquakes according to their intensity.

Mudslide Fast-moving stream of mainly soil and water caused by an earthquake.

Oceanic plate Tectonic plate under the ocean.

Peak wave Greatest height above land reached by a tsunami wave.

Plate boundary Edge of a tectonic plate.

Primary waves Also called P or pressure waves. The fastest shock waves and the first to be felt.

Richter scale A scale that measures earthquakes according to their magnitude.

'Ring of Fire' Name given to the area surrounding the Pacific Ocean where most of the world's earthquakes occur.

Shock waves The energy produced by an earthquake, which travels in waves through the earth. Also called seismic waves.

Secondary waves Also called S or shear waves. The second shock waves to be felt.

Seismometers Instruments which record the shock, or seismic waves of earthquakes. The records they produce are called seismographs.

Surface waves The slowest and most damaging shock waves, transporting the most energy.

Stress Pressure on underground rock caused when tectonic plates cannot move smoothly past one another.

Tsunami Powerful shock wave from an undersea earthquake that travels at high speed across the ocean, finally smashing into land.

Further Information

BOOKS

The Changing World: Earthquakes & Volcanoes edited by Steve Parker (Belitha, 1996)

Discoveries:Volcanoes and Earthquakes, edited by Dr Eldridge M. Moores (Macdonald Young Books, 1995)

Earthquakes and Volcanoes by Nicola Barber (Evans, 1998)

Focus on Disaster: Earthquake by Fred Martin (Heinemann, 1998)

Project Homework: Earthquakes by Jacqueline Dineen (Watts, 1995)

Restless Earth: Volcanoes & Earthquakes by Terry Jennings (Belitha, 1998)

Usborne Understanding Geography: Earthquakes & Volcanoes by F. Watt (Usborne, 1993)

Wonders of the World: Earthquakes by Neil Morris (Crabtree, 1999)

CD-ROMS

Earth Quest (Dorling Kindersley, 1997)

Violent Earth, (Wayland Multimedia, 1997) PC and MAC versions available. Looks at earthquakes, floods, hurricanes, tornadoes and duststorms as well as volcanoes.

WEB SITES

The world-wide web has hundreds of earthquake-related sites. Here are a few places to start:

United States Geological Survey (USGS) National Earthquake Information Centre www.geology.usgs.gov/quake.shtml www.neic.cr.usgs.gov

Environmental Change Research Centre, Department of Geography, UCL www.geog.ucl.ac.uk/ecrc

Benfield Greig Hazard Research Centre www.ucl.ac.uk/geolsci/research/ben-grei/

For information about the International Tsunami Survey Team (ITST): www.tsunami.civil.tohoku.ac.jp/hokusai2/news/PNG-result.html

Index

Page numbers in bold refer to photographs or illustrations.